CAPTAIN JOHN PAUL JONES

&

THE BATTLE OF

THE BONHOMME RICHARD

W M RHODES

Copyright © 2019 W M Rhodes

All rights reserved.

ISBN: 9781078268950

DEDICATION

This book is dedicated to the wonderful people of Filey who work tirelessly to keep Filey clean and tidy for us all to enjoy.

You know who you are.

All profits from the sale of this book go to Filey good causes.

Contents

ACKNOWLEDGMENTS vi

1 EARLY LIFE 1

2 COMING TO AMERICA 3

3 FURTHER TROUBLES 5

4 THE DANDY SKIPPER 6

5 THE FIGHT FOR INDEPENDENCE 9

7 CAPTAIN JOHN PAUL JONES 14

8 THE BONHOMME RICHARD 16

9 DUELLING DIFFERENCES 18

10 THE SERAPIS & CAPTAIN RICHARD PEARSON ... 20

11 LET BATTLE COMMENCE 21

12 CAPTAIN RICHARD PEARSON DEFENDS HIS ACTIONS 35

13. THE RETURNING HERO 38

APPENDIX - A BRIEF HISTORY OF AMERICA 43

John Paul Jones and The Battle of The Bonhomme Richard

ACKNOWLEDGMENTS

Thank you to all historian's past and present for making this small book possible.

***

"The eyes of all America are upon us. As we play our part posterity will bless or curse us."

– Henry Knox, officer of the Continental Army written after the *Declaration of Independence* in 1776

John Paul Jones and The Battle of The Bonhomme Richard

1 EARLY LIFE

The Battle of *The Bonhomme Richard* was fought off Filey Bay in September 1779 and for generations has been described as a memorable and intense battle, resulting in the events still being discussed over two centuries later. The central character of the story is Captain John Paul Jones, a little man who attracted the attention of two continents, and who in his brief career has earned him perpetual fame among the heroes of the world.

Wikimedia Commons

John Paul Jones and The Battle of The Bonhomme Richard

The house where John Paul Jones was born. Creative Commons Licence

John Paul (he added the Jones later, presumably as a tribute to his close friend and active American Revolutionary leader Willie Jones) was born of humble origin on the 6th July 1747, in a small white-washed cottage at Arbigland near Kirkbean, Kirkcudbrightshire, Scotland. He was the fifth child of seven children. His father was John Paul Snr a gardener for the Earl of Selkirk. His mother was Jean Mcduff (part of the McDuff clan). Neither of his parents registered their son's birth, which was not unusual for this era.

Living close to the sea, the young John Paul soon developed a spirit for seafaring and adventure. At the age of thirteen, he ran away to sea and signed up for a seven-year seaman's apprenticeship with the British ship called Friendship. His first voyage took him to Barbados and Fredericksburg in Virginia where he spent time with his elder brother William, who was a Tailor by profession who had emigrated there some years before and had flourished.

Being a sailor-suited John Paul, and he spent the next fourteen years sailing on various merchants and 'blackbirding' on slave ships between Britain, Virginia and the West Indies, learning the tactics of sea sailing and the art of navigation.

2 COMING TO AMERICA

Paul soon adopted America as his native country and considered England his enemy. In 1764, he was hired as 3rd mate on King George and two years later was promoted as 1st mate on *Two Friends.* A couple of years later, he participated in the transportation of slaves in ships that were totally unfit for humans. He hated this job and quit and described it as 'an abominable trade'

Luckily, for Paul, he got free passage home on the *'John'* a new ship from Kirkcudbright. It was during this voyage, that both the captain Samuel McAdam and the first mate died of a fever contracted in the West Indies. As the only qualified officer, the young Paul brought the ship safely back to its owners Corrie, Beck & Co who were so impressed with the young Captain that they appointed him master and gave him the role of supercargo for the ships next journey to America.

As captain of the *John*, he was very unpopular, and he would never get along with any of his crew, as he was generally disliked by the men who served with him. However, Jones respected the living conditions of his crew and prisoners, perhaps more than his contemporaries. If they disliked him, it was because he demanded from everyone, the same loyalty, and over-the-top effort that he himself provided without question. While others fought for God, family, and country, Jones apparently fought for Jones. Eventually, he managed to serve the cause of freedom with the same professionalism that he applied to transporting cargo and slaves.

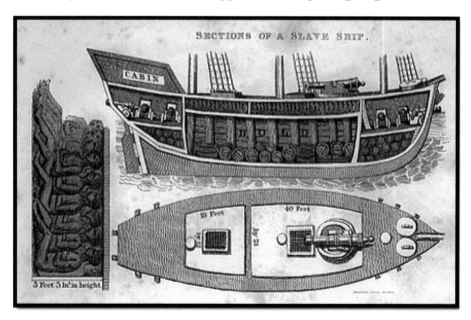

John Paul Jones and The Battle of The Bonhomme Richard

On his second voyage on the *John,* his infamous temper surfaced when he ordered the flogging of the ships carpenter Mungo Maxwell with a cat o nine tails. Maxwell was the son of one of Scotland's most prominent businessmen who disliked John Paul with a vengeance. Mungo Maxwell complained about his poor treatment while under Pauls' command. The carpenter was examined, and his injuries and his complaint were regarded as frolicsome. Unfortunately, on his next voyage on board the *Barcelona Packet* Maxwell died, his father complained to the authorities saying that his son was *'most mercifully wounded on his back as the result of flogging and this attributed to his untimely death.'*

Consequently, Paul was arrested, and when he returned to Kirkcudbright he was charged with murder. Fortunately for him, the captain of the *Barcelona Packet* produced evidence to show that the man died, not from his wounds, but from yellow fever whilst on another ship, and that when on joining his ship the man appeared to be in perfect health. Fortunately for Paul, he was acquitted. Soon after he was accepted as a freemason, a clear indication that few people in Kirkcudbright believed the charge. The story, however, dogged his entire life.

3 FURTHER TROUBLES

Cleared of those charges, he was embroiled in a second scandal in Tobago in 1773, when as Captain of *The Betsy* he chose not to pay his crew members. Justifiably, his then mutinous crew were so enraged that John Paul was forced to defend himself against the ringleader who he claimed attacked Jones in anger, Jones retaliated and struck him with a broadsword.

To defend his actions, John Paul wrote to Benjamin Franklin saying that he considered this incident to be the 'greatest misfortune of my life.' By his account, he immediately rowed ashore to the island of Tobago to turn himself into the Justice of the Peace. However, he was informed that he couldn't because no charges had been laid. He couldn't go before the Admiralty Court because the Admiralty judge was not on the island. So, he hopped on a horse and galloped from Scarborough to Courland Bay, where he caught a ship. From there, Paul disappeared, travelling incognito, as friends had advised, for fear of being extradited to Tobago to stand trial. In the winter of 1774, he surfaced as John Paul Jones in Virginia, where he had once visited his brother, who had since died.

4 THE DANDY SKIPPER

JONES, THE SOCIETY MAN
The picture which he himself liked best. From a miniature painted by Van der Huyt and presented by the naval hero to his royal patroness, the Duchess of Chartres. A copy of it is in the Hermitage Gallery, of St. Petersburg.

WikiCommons Licence

John Paul Jones was still poor and obscure but, he was in the right place at the right time and he quickly climbed the ranks within America's plight for independence. He soon became known as 'the dandy skipper' on account of his strong looks and gentlemanly manner. The ladies loved him and were impressed with his dashing swashbuckling reputation. His roving eye was legendary. Jones had a complex personality with an argumentative, narcissistic, quick and often violent temper, which would manifest itself throughout his career. Crew members hated him on account of his strictness and approach to ships standards and procedures.

Desperate to make his mark and fight against the British in the War for American Independence, Jones wrote to Joseph Hewes (the man who signed America's Declaration of Independence) to ask him personally for a naval appointment. In December 1775, John Paul Jones got his wish and he was appointed as a first Lieutenant in the newly formed Continental Navy.

The United States Declaration of Independence

The United States Declaration of Independence is the statement adopted by America following a meeting at the Pennsylvania State House, which is now Independence Hall in Philadelphia, on 4th July 1776.

The declaration declared that 13 colonies at war with Great Britain would consider themselves as 13 independent sovereign states and no longer under British rule. These 13 states took the first steps toward forming the United States of America as we know it today.

John Paul Jones and The Battle of The Bonhomme Richard

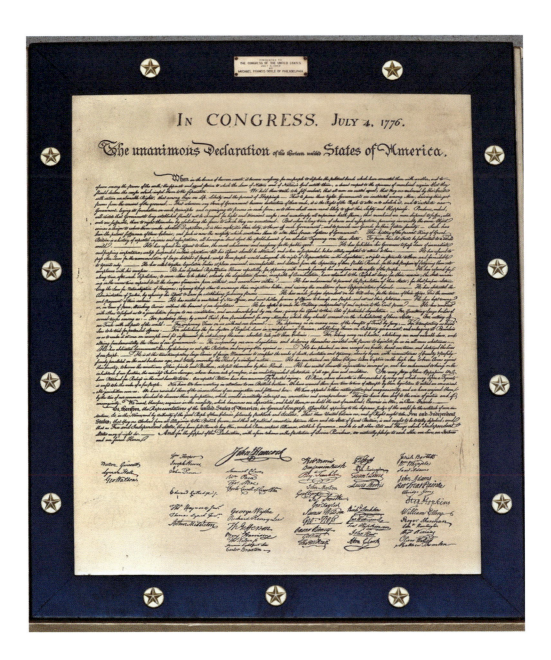

5 THE FIGHT FOR INDEPENDENCE

The American War of Independence was an armed conflict between Great Britain and thirteen of its former North American colonies. The conflict took place during the years 1775-1783, with the Declaration of Independence being issued on 4th July 1776. Relations between Britain and her American colonies had deteriorated following a British attempt to make the colonies contribute to the cost of their own defence, and those opposing this wanted to break free from constraints imposed by the British aristocracy. Fundamentalists, and radical politicians such as Sam Adams and Paul Revere, encouraged a break with Britain, whilst others hoped that this drastic action would be avoided.

WikiCommons Licence.

The descent into armed conflict between patriot (anti-British) and loyalist (pro-British) sympathisers was gradual. Events such as the Boston 'Massacre' of 1770, when British troops fired on a mob that had attacked a British sentry outside Boston's State House, and the Boston 'tea-party' of 1773, when British-taxed tea was thrown into the harbour were key turning points. Less obvious was the take-over of the colonial militias, which had initially been formed to defend against the French and the Native Americans. These units were run by officers in sympathy with the American patriots/rebels, rather than by soldiers in sympathy with pro-British loyalists. After initial clashes during 1775, the British landed 30,000 troops near New York in the summer of 1776 under General Howe. The city was taken, and the war began in earnest.

The Boston Tea Party Wikimedia Commons

6 PIRATES & PRIZES

JONES, THE "PIRATE."
Pictured as his foes regarded him. From a drawing made by a Britisher on the Serapis. Copies of it were printed and sold by the thousand throughout England.

WikiCommons Licence

With the American Navy in its infancy the country was very short of cash, and to fight their war for independence they needed a fleet of ships who would be powerful enough to stand up to the British Navy. For this purpose, the American Congress appointed approximately 1,700 privately owned warships to roam the ocean in quest

John Paul Jones and The Battle of The Bonhomme Richard

of British prizes.

When countries were at war 'Prizes' as they were referred to consisted of any enemy ship, either military or civilian which was considered fair game and could be captured as a prize. When this happened, the captain of the winning ship and its crew would share with the government any proceeds from the sale of the captured ships and their cargo.

The problem was that Britain was that at that time they did not consider America to be an independent nation, therefore Britain refused to give America the customary status of a nation at war.

At the time of the war, there were 1,700 privately owned warships roaming the ocean in quest of British prizes. Fundamentally, they were legalized pirates, these Revolutionary privateers carried congressional commissions that forbade attacks on neutral shipping and the mistreatment of captives but otherwise gave them free rein to rob and plunder the seas however they saw fit. Greed, as opposed to patriotism, was the normal driving force of these men who became privateers, which understandably generated anger and resentment among those serving in the Continental ranks. Privateers also gained a reputation for barbarism in combat that enraged the British and embarrassed many Americans.

John Paul Jones detested the way that Britain ignored the fight of the American's and he despised the way his native country simply ignored the customary rights at war of the new American Continental Navy, considering that they were nothing less than pirates and if captured Britain would toss them in jail like common criminals. It was this policy that Captain John Paul Jones wanted to change by attacking English Towns. His attacks on British ships were often sudden and secretive, and often bloody. To Britain, his use of that skill in covert military actions against his native country certainly led to his reputation as a pirate.

Although he was technically not a pirate or a privateer, Jones was often described as one. Working for Congress was the least profitable job of all. The early navy survived on this salary-plus-percentage formula. Jones was simply better at his job than most, although collecting his due was difficult. He survived most of his occupation with the US Navy without income, even paying for supplies with his own money. Eventually, Jones received a portion of his prize money. Because he did so and moved on, he is still seen by many as a highly efficient soldier of fortune.

John Paul Jones and The Battle of The Bonhomme Richard

7 CAPTAIN JOHN PAUL JONES

On 7th December 1775, Jones was appointed as 1st Lieutenant of the 24-gun frigate USS *Alfred* a small converted merchantman in the newly founded Continental Navy the flagship of Commodore Eske Hopkins. It was on this ship that he had the honour to become the first man to raise 'The Grand Union Liberty Flag'. There is also controversy as to whether this was the stars and stripes flag or the famous yellow silk banner with a rattlesnake, and perhaps a pine tree, emblazoned upon it, with the significant legend. 'Don't tread on me!'

Wikimedia Commons

Jones later Captained *'The Ranger'*, and in 1778 he and his crew crossed the Solway Frith from Whitehaven to Scotland, this time hoping to take for ransom the Earl of Selkirk (the very man his father had worked for). Jones' intention was to kidnap him and exchange him for American sailors who had been *impressed* into the Royal Navy. However, The Earl was not at home, only his wife the Countess and her young family. Disappointed, Jones and his crew made off with the silverware from the estate. Jones continued his journey raiding Whitehaven on the north-west coast of England and seeing action in Ireland and Scotland. (Earning the reputation of a 'pirate' in Britain.)

Jones' prowess on the sea earned him a promotion to Captain, and by January 1776 he was given the command of the sloop *Providence*. During her first cruise, *Providence* and her crew captured 16 British ships as prizes while harassing the British shipping industry around Nova Scotia. By November, Hopkins gave Jones command of *Alfred*, the larger ship. *Alfred* and *Providence*, with its new captain, headed toward the Bahamas, where they captured three British ships within a month. After eluding *HMS Milford* following a four-hour chase, *Alfred* returned to Boston and underwent a major refit. Jones was given command of *The Ranger* on July 14, 1777. Jones quickly sailed back to Europe, once more making audacious raids on England's shore. On Feb. 14, 1778, Jones' ship, *Ranger* was given the first salute from a foreign navy after the French signed an alliance treaty with the United States the week before.

8 THE BONHOMME RICHARD

Duc De Duras

WikiCommons Licence

Jones' exploits and success earned his command of the 42-gun frigate *The Bonhomme Richard*. Originally built in 1766 by the French East India Company. (La Compagnie des Indes) The frigate was formerly named *Duc de Duras*, a merchant ship which spent the first 13 years of her life ferrying cargo between France and the Orient. The ship was intended to be used for the new Continental Navy for use against Britain and was placed at the disposal of John Paul Jones on 4th February 1779, by King Louis XVI of France. The ship was financed with a loan to the United States by the French shipping magnate, Jacques-Donatien Le Ray de Chaumont, who historians consider to be the 'Father of the American Revolution'. As a compliment to Benjamin Franklin's almanack *'Poor Richard'* the ship was renamed *The Bonhomme Richard* (Good Man Richard). At the time that Jones took her command, the ship had already had four gruelling voyages to the Far East and back. This was not the type of ship Jones was expecting, having already declared 'I will have no connection with any ship that does not sail fast, for I intend to go in harm's way.'

Jones took command of the Bonhomme Richard from Monsieur Gabriel de Sartine the French Minister of Marine, in the spring of 1779. Initially, the *Duc de Duras* was designed as a two-decker with 32 guns, with two-gun decks which ran from bow to stern. However, Jones later adapted the ship to suit his needs. Jones hand-picked his officers, who despite Jones explosive temper and reputation for not getting on with his subordinates, for the most part, they respected their Captains leadership.

His crew were a different matter and according to a letter printed in *The London Chronicle* of the 28th September 1779, which states that most of Jones' crew were selected from the American colonies from different nationalities, many of them taken out of prisons at Brest and St. Malo. At that time, prisoners were offered their liberty on condition that they serve on Jones' fleet. However, they were treated as prisoners whilst on board. The article quotes: 'There were few Americans, some French and some neutrals such as Dutch and Germans'. It seems that this crew were at times rebellious and fought amongst themselves, at one time some crew members plotted to kill the Captain and take control of the ship. When Jones discovered this rebellious plot, he dismissed 100 English sailors and hauled the ringleader before a Court-Marshall. The punishment was 250 lashes. On another occasion, Jones had gone to shore, and the crew of his barge had deserted him to get drunk in town, he had to beg local fishermen to row him back to his ship. An outraged Jones saw that the crew were severally flogged upon their return for their insubordinate actions.

9 DUELLING DIFFERENCES

The journey began on 19th June 1779, from L'Orient, France with *The Bonhomme Richard* serving as the flagship, which also included *Alliance* an American 32 gun-frigate Captained by Pierre Landais. Landais was a French merchantman Lieutenant who trafficked much-needed arms to America. When he left the smuggling trade, he received a commission in the Continental Navy and given honouree citizenship of Massachusetts. He was then given command of the American warship *Alliance*-aptly named to recognise the new friendship between France and America. Landais was assigned to his ship to a squadron headed by Captain John Paul Jones.

 Initially, Jones and Landais relationship was affable, and Jones described Landais as a 'sensible well-informed man.' Unfortunately, this cordiality did not last long and in no time the pair had developed a deep dislike for each other that would last a lifetime.

John Paul Jones and The Battle of The Bonhomme Richard

Captain John Paul Jones & Captain Pierre Landis.

Library of Congress (Find a Grave)

10 THE SERAPIS & CAPTAIN RICHARD PEARSON

The English Captain Richard Pearson took a commission of *The Serapis* on 8th March 1779. Captain Richard Pearson1 was born in Appleby, Westmoreland in 1731. He entered the Navy in 1745 aged fourteen. Pearson was a Lieutenant during the Seven Years' War where he was very successful but was himself badly wounded in the conflict. He was subsequently unable to obtain a commission because his senior officers twice died before they could fulfil their promises. He finally received his commission as Captain in January 1773.

Serapis was launched from Deptford dockyard in March the same year. Named after the Greek God of fertility and afterlife, *Serapis* is described as having been an exceedingly fine ship with good sailing properties. *Serapis* was rated a 44-gun ship and mounted her guns on two complete decks. The present complement of the class was a trained man-of-war's crew of two hundred and eighty-five men.

11 LET BATTLE COMMENCE

Wikimedia Commons

For the American Navy Jones orders were simple. He was instructed to 'burn, sink or destroy all'. *The Bonhomme Richard*, together with four smaller vessels, *The Alliance, The Pallas, The Cerf,* and *The Vengeance*, of which only *The Alliance* and *The Cerf* were properly fitted for war, set sail from L'Orient on 19th June 1779, striking terror on their journey.

On 23rd September 1779 while *The Serapis* and *The Countess of Scarborough* were anchored under Scarborough Castle. Captain Pearson received intelligence that Jones and his American convoy were in Burlington Bay (Bridlington), which was a few leagues windward. The English ships departed keeping a watchful eye out for the American convoy and the notorious Commodore John Paul Jones. Around six in the evening, it was all hands to quarters, as four vessels came into sight. *The Serapis* made the signal to *The Countess of Scarborough* to stay close to their stern. English colours were hoisted on both ships.

The wind was slight that evening as the American ships came up very slowly.

John Paul Jones and The Battle of The Bonhomme Richard

Captain Pearson instructed that the ports in the lower deck were to be down. This was meant as a decoy. However, the enemy was far too cunning and soon saw through this. At about seven-thirty, the enemy ships bore close and hoisted American colours, but it was so dark that they were presumed to be the colours of St. George, and orders were given on pain of death not to fire. To be certain, Captain Pearson hailed her, and believed the response to be *'Princess Amelia.'* He hailed again with the warning: 'If you do not tell us clearly from whence you came, we will fire you (now they were very close, within half a pistol shot, but it was too dark to recognise their colours). Suddenly, there was a flash of gunfire in one of the lower decks, *The Serapis* responded instantaneously by giving them a broadside. Initially, it was clear that *The Serapis* had superior firepower. However, Jones chose to fight at close range to overcome his disadvantage. The ships were so close that the nozzles of the guns touched as the vessels rolled on heavy seas.

There was no time to be lost, the enemy was all too close, every shot told. There was no choice but to haul the dead and wounded from the guns and to fire and load at the same time.

Wikimedia Commons

By this time, a huge crowd of people had gathered on the cliffs and on the shore to watch the battle by the light of the rising moon. Some of the gunfire was so near that a few canon-balls grazed Flamborough's white cliffs. For the next two hours firing continued, with many deaths on both sides with people jumping ships to save themselves, Jones managed to carry away the jibboom from *The Serapis* (to ensure they would not sail off too far). *The Bonhomme Richard's* bow and *The Serapis* touched, and as fast as they could each raise the guns, shots were fired.

Wikimedia Commons

Gradually, *The Serapis* shot away the entire side of *The Bonhomme Richard,* which was riddled like a sieve, causing the ship to take in several feet of water in the hold. Her rotten sides were almost blown out to starboard and port by the batteries of the Serapis. Captain Pearson was a brave man, but he was no match for the indomitable personality of the Scottish would be American Commander. After several hours of fighting, he asked Jones if he wanted to strike (surrender) to which Jones is reported to have replied with the famous words, 'I have not yet begun to fight.' Reports state that unlike the honourable Captain Pearson, Jones would have sunk the ship, men, and himself, before he would have 'struck.' When told that *The Bonhomme Richard* was sinking Jones said, 'let her sink and be damned, she cannot be in a better place than alongside an English man-of-war!' Some of Jones' crew cried out 'we have struck' and *The Serapis* Boatswain went on board *The Bonhomme Richard* to take possession of her, he was met with a Frenchman's small sword in his groin, and another through his brain, he fell back onto the Serapis where he died instantly.

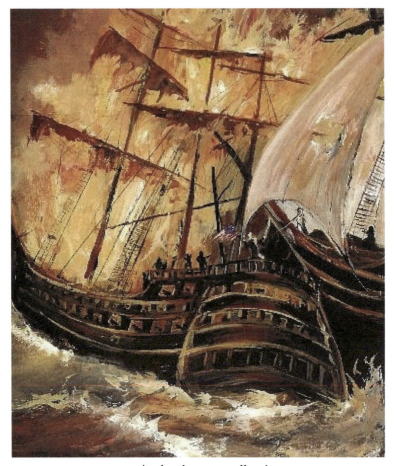

Author's own collection

The Bonhomme Richard's damaged gun decks were barely capable of fighting, it was a terrible scene, there were dead lying on the living, there were men without arms and some without legs, many were bleeding to death as two of the three doctors were dead and there were no bandages or dressings left. Yet still, with Jones' leadership and determination, the remaining crew fought on through the night.

John Paul Jones and The Battle of The Bonhomme Richard

On Board The Bonhomme Richard

As the water rose in *The Bonhomme Richard* fear set into the mind of John Burbank her master-at-arms, consequently, he took pity on the crying prisoners who were trapped in the hole with water rising around them, so without orders, Burbank opened the hatches and released the British prisoners caught in previous actions. Jones was furious and instantly put the exhausted men to work manning the sinking ship's water pumps. These prisoners were terrified but grateful to have been set free. They could have quite easily tipped the balance against the Americans, and they could have all bolted and jumped ship, shot Jones or thrown him overboard, but surprisingly most of them stayed put. Perhaps they were more concerned with saving themselves from imminent drowning or being shot on the spot, but because of their actions, they became an integral part of the subsequent American victory.

Wikimedia Commons

Nevertheless, a few did escape taking advantage of the confusion and made their escape to Filey, where they were made prisoner and taken before Humphrey Osbaldeston, at Hunmanby.

John Paul Jones and The Battle of The Bonhomme Richard

John Paul Jones capturing the *Serapis* engraving by Alonzo Chappel

Once again Captain Pearson called Jones to strike, or he must infallibly sink to the bottom. Jones replied, 'I may sink, but I'll be damned if I strike!' At this time one of Jones' crew attempted to strike the colours but Jones turned around and shot him dead on the spot, another two attempted and suffered the same fate. A mutiny was expected to take place as the ship was sinking when one of Jones' squadron immediately came to his assistance which turned the tables on the Serapis. *The Bonhomme Richard* was in such a bad way. The rudder was gone, the stern frame and stanchions were cut away, the timbers of the lower deck from the mainmast to stern were mangled beyond description, dying men were lying in pools of blood and groaning piteously.

The ship was burning in several places, and the water in the hold was rising steadily. Realising that *The Bonhomme Richard* was sinking and the seriousness of the situation, Jones still fought doggedly on, until the mizzenmast of the Serapis went by the board, whereupon Captain Pearson called for quarter, and Jones then ordered a boarding crew onto *The Serapis,* and against all odds captured The Serapis and its crew, where they triumphantly raised their country's colours. *The Countess of Scarborough* suffered a similar fate as she surrendered to *The Pallas* and the *Alliance*.

Wikimedia Commons

Many lives were lost on both sides of the conflict. This is an account of the ship's men, and guns prior to engagement.

John Paul Jones and The Battle of The Bonhomme Richard

The American's Capt. Jones	Guns	Men
Bonhomme Richard - Jones	44	380
Pallas-Cpt Cottineau	32	320
Alliance-Cpt Landais	36	300
Vengeance	12	100
TOTAL	124	1100
THE ENGLISH	Guns	Men
The Serapis-Captain Pearson	44	285
The Countess of Scarborough	20	100
TOTAL	64	385

Therefore, it was clear that from the beginning of the battle Jones had three times more men than the English (715) and 60 more guns.

Accounts from the time show that the loss of life on both sides was horrendous and as follows:

The Bonhomme Richard – 250 men killed and wounded.

The Pallas – 6 men and 1 Lieutenant killed, with many wounded.

The Alliance – nobody killed and 2 wounded.

John Paul Jones and The Battle of The Bonhomme Richard

The English

The Serapis – 125 killed and wounded.

The Countess of Scarborough – 30 killed and wounded.

Total loss of life on both sides: 411.

Two days later between the hours of ten and eleven on the morning of 25th September, *The Bonhomme Richard* drifted towards Filey Bay where she eventually sank, her flag flying as she went down. Nothing of her was saved except her signal flag. John Paul Jones and his victorious crew and prizes sailed *Serapis and The Countess of Scarborough* along with Captain Pearson and his crew as hostages to Texel in the Netherlands where Jones sought safe harbour and much-needed repairs.

The Serapis was the first British vessel ever to be captured by an American ship, causing British fears of an invasion fleet being dispatched from across the Atlantic. The English were exasperated at the humiliation suffered by the total defeat of one of their best frigates. Sir Joseph Yorke, British Ambassador, wrote to the Dutch on behalf of the King of England to protest at Jones' conduct saying that, '*The Serapis* and *The Countess of Scarborough* and their Captains and crew were attacked and taken by force by John Paul Jones who had received no commission from his own country. Therefore, to the treaties and laws of war, Jones falls under the classification of Rebels and Pirates.' The Dutch did not agree to the Ambassador's request, stating that they would prefer to 'observe neutrality.' On 7th October, Jones left the ship and went to Amsterdam. Captain Pearson was kept as a hostage and finally released on 21st November 1779 in exchange for Captain Gustave Conyngham, whom the British were holding prisoner.

The capture of the Serapis. Grainger-Authors own collection.

John Paul Jones and The Battle of The Bonhomme Richard

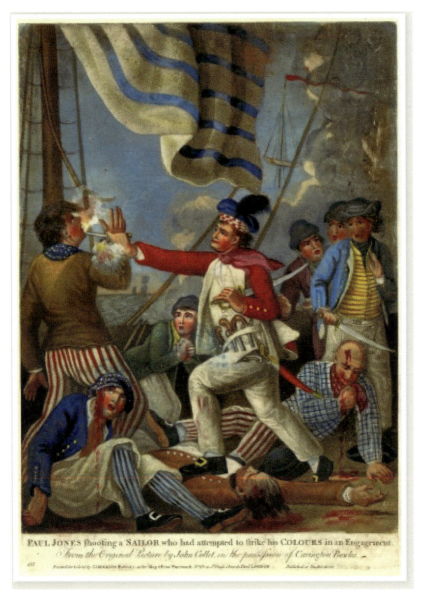

Paul Jones shooting a Sailor who had attempted to strike his Colours (Bowles from John Collet, 1779), British Museum.

Captain Jones was not at all happy with the actions of his master-at-arms John Burbank and he insisted that he be put in irons for liberating prisoners during the conflict.

On 3rd October 1780, Captain Pearson was honourably acquitted by a Court Martial for the loss of the *Serapis* and was instead knighted by the King of England for his services to this most famous battle. When Jones was told of this, he is reported to have said: 'Never mind, if I meet him again, I'll make a Lord of him!' Captain Pearson died in 1806 at The Royal Naval Hospital in Greenwich, where he was Lieutenant Governor.

The French ordered Captain Cottineau de Kerlogeun to take command of *The Serapis* in the Texel and bring her back to France. Subsequently, *The Serapis* was refitted for the French Navy and under Captain Roche sent to assist in a campaign to wrest India from British rule. Roche proceeded to the French fort, Île Sainte-Marie located off the northern coast of Madagascar. While Roche was ashore, a lieutenant and a subordinate went below deck to obtain the daily brandy ration for the sailors. While the men were 'cutting' the brandy's full strength with water, their lantern fell into the vat and set the spirit locker on fire. Attempts to extinguish the blaze failed and after two-and-a-half hours, the flames burned through the locker walls and reached the powder magazine. An explosion blew out the stern and the vessel sank.

Analogous to the wreck of *The Bonhomme Richard*, the whereabouts of *The Serapis* was for many years' unknown. However, in November 1999 it was discovered by American nautical archaeologist, Richard Swete and his associate Michael Tuttle. After many years of research and a systematic magnetometer survey of the harbour on Île Sainte-Marie, Swete and a team of archaeologists finally discovered the remains of the *Serapis*.

12 CAPTAIN RICHARD PEARSON DEFENDS HIS ACTIONS

In a letter dated 14th October 1779, Captain Richard Pearson gives his account of the battle, in which he states:

'On my going on board *The Bonhomme Richard*. I found her in great distress, her quarters and counter on the lower deck entirely drove in, and the whole of her lower decks dismounted, she was also on fire in two places with six or seven feet of water in her hold which increased throughout the night and into the next day until we

Wikimedia Commons

were obliged to quit her and she sank, with a great number of wounded people on board. She had 306 men killed and wounded in the action. I am sorry for losing his majesty's ship that I had the honour to command, but at the same time, I flatter myself with the hopes, that their Lordships will be convinced that she has not been given away, but on the contrary, that every exertion has been used to defend her,

Captain Richard Pearson Wikimedia Commons

and that two essential pieces of service to our country has arisen from it. The one is wholly oversetting the crews of this flying squadron, the other is referring the whole of a valuable convoy into the hands of the enemy, which I believe would have been the case had I acted other than the way I did.

13. THE RETURNING HERO

Despite being venerated today; John Paul Jones was never promoted to a rank higher than that of Captain in the American Navy. Strangely enough, he did become an admiral in 1788. However, ironically it was in Russia's Black Sea fleet, at the invitation of Empress Catherine II. He was also appointed US Consul to Algiers in 1792, but he never got the chance to take up this position, as on 18th July 1792, John Paul Jones was found dead face down on his bed at his residence at Rue de Tournon in Paris. He was forty-five years old. The cause of death was kidney failure.

John Paul Jones was buried in Paris at the Saint Louis Cemetery, which belonged to the French Royal Family. Four years later, France's revolutionary government sold the property and the cemetery was forgotten. Jones's body was preserved in alcohol and interred in a lead coffin just in case the United States decided to claim his remains, they might more easily be identified.

This is exactly what happened, as after a lengthy search, Jones' body was located, and his remains were exhumed and taken back to America.

On 24th April 1906, Jones' coffin was installed in Bancroft Hall at the United States Naval Academy, Annapolis, Maryland. On 26th January 1913, the Captain's remains were finally re-interred in a magnificent bronze and marble casket at the Naval Academy Chapel in Annapolis. John Paul Jones is the father of The American Navy.

The house in Paris where John Paul Jones died Author's own Collection

John Paul Jones and The Battle of The Bonhomme Richard

Wikimedia Commons

| At the time of writing this book, the search for the wreckage of *The Bonhomme Richard* continues, and while there does continue to be reported sightings, which hopefully will come to fruition and bring an end to the mystery of this most famous ship's final resting-place. Finding what is left if anything of the wreckage cannot be an easy task, after all, this was an ageing ship (it was 14 years old before it sank) that has been at the bottom of the sea for over two hundred and forty years.

Furthermore, it was constructed of timber and badly damaged and it was on fire prior to sinking. If located it would be a tremendous find for the American's and a massive boost to tourism in the Yorkshire area, putting Filey and the Yorkshire Coast firmly at the centre of American history, and an integral part of its fight for freedom and Independence.

John Paul Jones and The Battle of The Bonhomme Richard

APPENDIX - A BRIEF HISTORY OF AMERICA

Long before the pilgrim fathers established what is now America. A man named Lucas Vazquez de Ayllon a Spanish magistrate and explorer who on the festival of Saint Michael, September 29, 1526 established a colony in Carolina known as San Miguel de Gualdape. This colony was the first European attempt at a settlement in what is now the United States. This settlement was short lived as after only three months many Spaniards died of either disease, cold, hunger or trouble with the natives. The remaining survivors left (150 out of initial settlers of 6-700 people). Ayllon died in Virginia from fever in 1526, before his death he gave an account of the region, which inspired numerous attempts by the Spanish and French governments to colonize the southeastern United States. Interestingly, Ayllon is recorded as the first person to bring black slaves to North America, an attempt that failed and occasioned the first slave rebellion.

In 1578 Englishman Sir Humphrey Gilbert gained permission from the Virgin Queen, Queen Elizabeth the establish a colony in America, he sailed to Newfoundland, but soon abandoned his venture, Gilbert was lost on his return home.

Gilbert's half-brother Walter Raleigh attempted to establish a settlement there in 1584 when he set sail with two ships to America. Queen Elizabeth gave him permission to name the place Virginia after her (The Virgin Queen). A year later, an expedition led by Richard Grenville left men on Roanoke Island, he then returned to England to recruit settlers and obtain further supplies. Whilst he was gone, the settlers on the island ran short of supplies, so they abandoned Virginia and returned to England.

A man named John White, was the next person to bring men, women and children to Virginia in 1587. However, once again the settlers soon ran short of supplies, so White returned to England. Unfortunately, due to a war between England and Spain he was unable to return. It is not documented what happened to the colonists he left behind in Virginia.

JAMESTOWN AND VIRGINIA

Gentlemen adventures decided to join together to pool their resources and find a colony in North America. This amalgamation proved successful and in 1606, the Virginia Company was founded. These intrepid explorers sent two expeditions to North America. Raleigh Gilbert (Sir Humphrey Gilbert's son) led one of them. They landed in Maine but soon gave up. They returned to England in 1609. The second expedition founded Jamestown on 14 May 1607.

More settlers arrived in 1609. However, as their predecessors found the shortage of food, disease, and conflict with the natives caused many deaths among the colonists.

By the year 1610 the survivors were on the verge of leaving. They were dissuaded from doing so only when more ships from England arrived. In 1611 Sir Thomas Dale became the Governor of the colony. He introduced strict discipline with a code of laws called 'Laws, Divine, Moral and Martial'. Penalties for disobedience were severe.

In 1612, a man named John Rolfe started to grow tobacco, and the industry of Virginia prospered. The first Virginian tobacco was sold in England in 1614, this then became the mainstay of the Virginia economy.

Gradually the colony expanded. In 1618 the Company offered 50 acres of land to anyone who could pay for the cost of their voyage across the Atlantic. If they could not pay, they could become indentured servants. When they had to work for the company for several years to pay back the cost of their passage. In 1619 the first slaves arrived in Virginia. Also, in 1619, the first representative government in North America was created when the House of Burgesses met.

In 1624 the Virginia Company was dissolved, and the Crown took over the colony. By 1660 the population of Virginia was 27,000. By 1710 it had risen to 78,000. However, in 1699 the seat of government of Virginia was moved from Jamestown to Middle Plantation (Williamsburg). Afterward, Jamestown went into decline. (Source. A short history of the USA. Tim Lambert.)

THE PILGRIM FATHERS

By 1620, a group of English separatists established a colony in the 'New World.' These separatists were disillusioned with The Church of England and migrated to America to be able to establish a community to practice their religion, whilst still retaining their English identity.

ABOUT THE AUTHOR

Wendy has written four other books;

Filey A History of the Town and its People.

Dr Pritchard the Poisoning Adulterer

Scarborough A History of the Town and its People

Bloody Yorkshire (13 Crimes from Bygone Times)

Coming Soon (2020) Bloody Yorkshire Volume 2.

Wendy started her working life working for Bradford Libraries, she moved to Filey in the early 1990's with her husband.

She studied BA (Hons) English Literature with The Open University, and later gained a master's degree in English Literature & Creative Writing at Teesside University.

She now lives in Spain with her husband two dogs and four cats.

Printed in Great Britain
by Amazon